# The end of history and
# the beginning of education

INSTITUTE OF EDUCATION

University of London

# The end of history and the beginning of education

## Richard Aldrich

Professor of the History of Education

Based on an Inaugural Lecture
delivered at the Institute of Education,
University of London on 12 March 1997

First published in 1997 by the Institute of Education
University of London, 20 Bedford Way, London WC1H 0AL
Tel: 0171-580 1122. Fax: 0171-612 6126

*Pursuing Excellence in Education*

© Institute of Education University of London 1997

British Library Cataloguing in Publication Data:
a catalogue record for this publication is available
from the British Library

ISBN 0 85473-514-3

---

Typography and design by Joan Rose

Produced in Great Britain by Reprographic Services
Institute of Education University of London

Printed by Formara Limited
16 The Candlemakers, Temple Farm Industrial Estate
Southend on Sea, Essex SS2 5RX

I1-0010-BMIL-0297

## Acknowledgments

I am very pleased to have this opportunity to thank Averil Aldrich and other members of my family for their support over many years.

I should also like to express my gratitude to colleagues past and present. Particular thanks are due to David Crook, who commented on an earlier version of the text with his customary wisdom and tact, and to Deborah Spring and Joan Rose for seeing the text into print.


*Richard Aldrich*
*January 1997*

*Professor Richard Aldrich*

Indeed, many of the lessons to be drawn from historical perspectives upon education must be couched in terms of caution, of thorough research and planning, of emphasizing the need above all to retain that which is good while seeking to improve that which is of less worth. A clear example of this is provided by school buildings, which represent one of the most important forms of evidence from the past. Indeed, one of the greatest weaknesses of some writers *about* history, as opposed to writers *of* history, is their excessive concentration upon verbal artefacts and narrative prose discourses. School buildings represent in a most tangible way, priorities and beliefs about a variety of elements of education, including such intangibles as the nature of childhood and society, of pedagogical purposes and practices. Many of these buildings are still being used – decades, centuries even, after they were constructed. They provide a physical context for the education of the children of today and of tomorrow. Some of them are better adapted to the purposes of education than others, and it is a shame upon us all that some of the worst school buildings date from the 1960s and 1970s. In common with some of the homes constructed at that time, they were, and remain, manifestly unfit for the purposes for which they were intended.

This is, or should be, a sobering thought. The mistakes and meanness of policy makers in education may be visited not only upon the children of one generation, but even upon those of their children's children. This is not only true in respect of buildings. It also applies to curriculum and pedagogy.

In 1990, in a rare moment of public self-doubt, Margaret Thatcher acknowledged this as she began to understand the problems that her government's interventions in respect of the school history curriculum were producing:

> Now the History Report has come out. It is very detailed. There were not many secondary school teachers on the syllabus-forming committee. I think it really must be put out to great consultation and consideration. My worry is whether we should put out such a detailed one. You see, once you put out an approved curriculum, if you have got it wrong, the situation is worse afterwards than it was before. At any given time a large

> number of teachers are teaching a subject extremely well. But
> if you take them off what they know has worked for years, far
> better than anyone else's syllabus, then you wonder: were you
> doing it right? (Quoted in Aldrich 1991: 3)

Just so Prime Minister. Nevertheless, in spite of these doubts, Margaret
Thatcher made innumerable interventions in respect of the history
curriculum. Kenneth Baker has a history degree and a continuing interest
in the subject, but as Margaret Thatcher explained in her memoirs:

> Though not an historian myself, I had a very clear – and I had
> naively imagined uncontroversial – idea of what history was.
> History was an account of what happened in the past. Learning
> History, therefore, requires knowledge of events. (Thatcher
> 1993: 595)

This is a useful definition as far as it goes, but, as indicated in the first
section, it is deficient in at least two respects. First, there is no single account
of what happened in the past. As the recent plethora of memoirs from retired
and ousted politicians clearly demonstrates, there are many such accounts.
Second, these accounts do not always agree, even when (perhaps particularly
when) they are written by people who participated in the very events they
are recounting. Margaret Thatcher's idea of history was a primitive one,
but on the basis of that understanding she confidently proceeded, as she
tells us herself, to reject Secretary of State, Kenneth Baker's original list
of members of the History Working Group and the guidance to be offered
to them, and subsequently to overrule the proposed responses both of Baker
and of his successor, John MacGregor, to the interim and final History
reports.

  It is to be hoped that some lessons have been learned from the tortuous,
time-consuming, expensive and irrational exercise of producing a national
curriculum for schools. Unfortunately, several government interventions
in the field of education have provided clear examples of the predominance
of ideology over truth, examples which Michael Barber has recently
characterized as 'Free-Market Stalinism' (Barber 1996: 55-60).

# The end of history

In 1989 a 15-page article written by Francis Fukuyama and entitled 'The End of History?' was published in the journal, *National Interest* (Fukuyama 1989). This was to be followed in 1992 by the substantial tome entitled *The End of History and the Last Man* (Fukuyama 1992).

Fukuyama's thesis attracted much attention. Few professional historians agreed with it fully, but the fact that his many critics felt it necessary to explain their objections, coupled with the overthrow of Communist or Socialist regimes in central and eastern Europe which seemed to endorse his interpretation, brought Fukuyama and his ideas centre stage.

Fukuyama went back to Hegel to resurrect the idea that history, as a process in human existence, had a beginning and an end. History began with the discovery that people might be free, and would end once human beings had discovered the rational way of organizing their affairs to achieve that end. The events of 1989-92 indicated that history had ended, in the sense that liberal democracy had become generally, though not universally, recognized as the best means of government. Fukuyama's thesis depended upon his particular definition of history. Of course, he did not mean that the normal process of human events would come to an end, nor that such events would become a past which historians and others would decline to study. His question was:

> Whether, at the end of the twentieth century, it makes sense for us once again to speak of a coherent and directional History of mankind that will eventually lead the greater part of humanity to liberal democracy? The answer I arrive at is yes, for two separate reasons. One has to do with economics, and the other has to do with what is termed the 'struggle for recognition.' (Fukuyama 1992: xii-xiii)

Fukuyama argued that 'Looking around the world there remains a very strong overall correlation between advancing socio-economic modernization and the emergence of new democracies' (Fukuyama, 1992: 112). But although the desire for a better standard of living and a market economy was a crucial factor in the revolutions which challenged or overthrew

Communist regimes, equal importance in Fukuyama's analysis was to be given to an idea – the idea of recognition. In a chapter entitled 'On the Possibility of Writing a Universal History', published in 1995, he stated that:

> people did not go into the streets of Leipzig, Prague, Timisoara, Beijing or Moscow demanding that the government give them a postindustrial economy. Their passionate anger was aroused over their perceptions of injustice which had nothing to do with economics . . . In the accounts of the resistance in St Petersburg to the hardline coup in August 1991, those who rallied to the side of the 'democrats' . . . demanded less a market economy than a government that recognized their elementary rights under a rule of law, a government that did not lie to them about the crimes and stupidities it had committed in the past, that would allow them freely to express their thymotic opinions about right and wrong, and that would ultimately treat them not as children but as adults capable of governing themselves. (Fukuyama 1995a: 25)

Several arguments may be advanced against Fukuyama's notion of an end of history. Many states, including China, potentially the most powerful of all, are far from being liberal democracies. Authoritarian regimes flourish in many parts of the world. National, racial, ethnic and religious ideologies remain strong, and in the face of such ideologies liberal principles and economic well-being may count for little, not only in countries of the so-called Third World, but even in Europe itself, as in the former Yugoslavia.

Liberal democracies are also threatened from within. In some liberal democracies, including the United Kingdom, on occasion citizens may be deprived of their rights and treated like children, while governments can and do cover up past mistakes and crimes. Meanwhile the rich get richer and the poor get poorer. For example, in the United States 'in 1989 the top 1% earned more collectively than the bottom 40%' (Handy 1996: 34). There is considerable evidence that we live in a society characterized by a breakdown in family and in family values, the emergence of an unemployed, possibly an unemployable, underclass, a rapid escalation in the use of drugs and in the incidence of violent crime. Consumerism prevails, with a new cultural imperialism based upon such universal values as McDonalds and Coca Cola.

Nevertheless, the concept of the end of history raises a number of important points for the historian of education and for the application of historical perspectives, four of which will be considered here. These relate to historiography, education, ideology and language.

The first issue is to locate Fukuyama's thesis within a historiographical context. In one sense his argument is simply a rather grandiose comment upon the long observed bankruptcy – ideological and material – of certain political regimes. In some senses it replicates the analyses of such writers as Herbert Marcuse and Daniel Bell. Other links may be made with the writings of Karl Popper. The first volume of *The Open Society and its Enemies*, published in 1945, was inscribed 'In memory of the countless men and women . . . who fell victims to the Fascist and Communist belief in Inexorable Laws of Historical Destiny'. A further connection may be observed with the work of J.H. Plumb. In a volume entitled *The Death of the Past*, based upon the Saposnekow lectures given at the City College, New York in March 1968, Plumb distinguished between history and the past, arguing in support of rational, professional historians who would create 'an historical past, objective and true' (Plumb 1969: 16). In contrast, Plumb opposed that past which he depicted as having flourished in a variety of totalitarian cultures, including China across the ages, and the USSR of his own day. This he characterized as 'a created ideology with a purpose, designed to control individuals, or motivate societies, or inspire classes' (Plumb 1969: 17). He even predicted that 'Russia cannot detach itself from the West. The dogma of history, as now practised in Russia, is unlikely to remain in its present form for many more decades. Soon Russia and her satellites will be facing the problem of a past corroded by the practice of history' (Plumb 1969: 104).

Where does the concept of the end of history stand in relation to postmodernist historical interpretations? In one sense the end of history appears to be essentially modernist, in so far as it provides a logical interpretation of the development of human events, in Fukuyama's terms 'the end point of ideological evolution'. On the other hand, postmodernists may identify the end of history with the end of certaintist histories, the final demise of the great metanarratives. In the words of Jenkins, 'we have reached the end of modernist versions of what history is' (Jenkins 1995: 35). Much depends upon whether the end of history is to be interpreted as the end of modernist versions of history or rather as the confirmation of such history.

A second theme is that of the place of education within this framework. Although *The End of History* contains a chapter entitled 'In the Land of Education' (Fukuyama 1992: 109-125), Fukuyama's comments upon the relationship between education and his principal theme are both minimal and tentative. After the briefest of treatments he concludes simply that

> It is reasonably clear that education is, if not an absolutely necessary precondition, then at least a highly desirable adjunct to democracy. It is hard to imagine democracy working properly in a largely illiterate society where the people cannot take advantage of information about the chances open to them. But it is a rather different matter to say that education *necessarily* leads to belief in democratic norms. (Fukuyama 1992: 122)

Fukuyama's concentration upon the possible role of education in *promoting* democracy, however, should not preclude an identification of other issues concerning outcomes. Since education, as represented by such dimensions as organization, assessment, curriculum and pedagogy, both reflects values concerning society as it is, and as those who control it (and others) would wish it to be, any generalization of liberal democracy must affect the nature and purposes of provided education. More fundamentally still, if the end of history is to be accompanied by an end to some basic ideological struggles and a focus upon the nature and quality of liberal democracy, governments will have more reason and time to concentrate upon economic and social concerns, including education. Thus a Soviet regime which put a man into space has been displaced by a Russian one which places a higher priority upon getting steak and razor blades into Moscow. In the United Kingdom the role of Secretary of State for Education and Employment may become more important than that of Secretary of State for Foreign Affairs. A more universal acceptance of liberal democracy, moreover, may diminish the nostalgia for hierarchical educational forms associated with an imperial past. Such processes will be influenced in the United Kingdom, as elsewhere, by the increased participation within liberal democracies of the members of that half of the human race who have for so long been excluded from political and professional power.

The third point concerns the ideological positions from which history, and in this context particularly history of education, is studied and written. From its modern origins in the later nineteenth century much British history of education was written in a broadly celebratory style – in which the rise of a national system of free and compulsory schooling was centre stage. This interpretation was challenged in the 1960s and 1970s by such historians as Richard Johnson, Brian Simon and Charles Webster. These writers, far from celebrating the achievements of the British educational system, characterized it as inegalitarian and heavily bureaucratized, a system specifically designed to fail the majority of children. From 1979, Conservative governments, politicians and think tanks also expressed serious criticisms of state education. Their analysis of the situation, however, was not based upon the interpretations of such historians as Johnson, Simon and Webster, but rather upon those of E.G. West, Martin Wiener and Correlli Barnett. West's delineation of the achievements of British education before the establishment of school boards in 1870, and his fundamental questioning of the role of the state, could be used to provide a rationale for the limitation of the role of local education authorities, and for the promotion of diversity in institutions and consumer choice (West 1970). Wiener's study of English culture and the long decline of the industrial spirit after 1851, quoted with approval Edward Heath's warning in 1973 that,

> The alternative to expansion is not, as some occasionally seem
> to suppose, an England of quiet market towns linked only by
> trains puffing slowly and peacefully through green meadows.
> The alternative is slums, dangerous roads, old factories, cramped
> schools, stunted lives. (Wiener 1981: 162)

Even more influential was the savage indictment of British industrial and educational policies and standards contained in Correlli Barnett's, *The Audit of War*. Barnett concluded that in the aftermath of the second world war the dreams of 1945 would fade one by one – the imperial and Commonwealth role, the world power role, British industrial genius, and, at the last, New Jerusalem itself, a dream turned to a dank reality of a segregated, subliterate, unskilled, unhealthy and institutionalised proletariat hanging on the nipple of state maternalism. (Barnett 1986: 304)

From the mid 1980s historians of education in the United Kingdom could not but be excited, mesmerised even, by the amount of history of education that was being created before their very eyes. Such changes, however, were part of a broader pattern. Even before the revolutions in central and eastern Europe, and the emergence of the concept of the end of history, two phenomena were becoming apparent in British politics. The first was the decline in numbers of the traditional working classes, and of working-class occupations. The second was that the social and economic agenda of the Left – nationalization, high levels of taxation on the rich, an ever increasing welfare state, a powerful trade union movement – was losing its appeal.

For historians of education, therefore, the effect upon ideological positioning produced by the concept of the end of history was compounded by the ending of the traditional (or indeed mythical) working classes. Perspectives were changing. As David Marquand noted in *The Progressive Dilemma: from Lloyd George to Kinnock* (1991), 'Conservative or predominantly Conservative governments have been in office for fifty of the seventy-odd years since the Labour Party first became the official opposition in the House of Commons, and Labour governments for only twenty' (quoted in Clarke 1992: 60). There was only one great period of Labour success and, as has been observed by such commentators as Peter Clarke, the victory of 1945 was the product not of a particular commitment to socialist policies, but rather of a general post-war belief that there was a need for radical social and economic change, a belief which prevailed across the boundaries of social class (Clarke 1992: 60).

Such re-examination has the widest national and international implications. The industrial proletariat of England has a particular significance in discussions about the end of history, for it was the English urban proletariat which provided evidence for the theories of Marx and Engels. The relative alienation of this proletariat from socialism, from the

Labour party and from the system of state-provided schooling, is a phenomenon which merits considerable further analysis. One starting point for such analysis is the idea that the key divisions in nineteenth- and twentieth-century British society were not only between upper, middle and working classes, but also between the religious and respectable of all classes on the one hand, and the irreligious and disreputable on the other (Laqueur 1976).

The final point in this section extends the implications of the concept of the end of history from the ideological positions from which history of education is written to the very language which such historians employ. Given the probability that varieties of history (including those of a postmodernist kind) are more likely to flourish in liberal democracies than in many other types of states, it is difficult to predict their nature with any certainty. The proliferation or consolidation of liberal democracies will not bring an end to disputes between conservatives and radicals, traditionalists and progressives, whether amongst historians or educationists, albeit such rivalries may be conducted within narrower parameters. Marxist and neo-Marxist positions, however, have been considerably weakened, if not rendered untenable. It may, therefore, be necessary both to abandon such historical positions and perspectives, and even to discard their very concepts and terminology. In an important recent chapter Richard Rorty has suggested that

> I think the time has come to drop the terms 'capitalism' and 'socialism' from the political vocabulary of the left. It would be a good idea to stop talking about 'the anticapitalist struggle' and to substitute something banal and untheoretical – something like 'the struggle against avoidable human misery'. More generally, I hope that we can banalize the entire vocabulary of leftist political deliberation. I suggest that we start talking about greed and selfishness rather than about bourgeois ideology, about starvation wages and lay-offs rather than about the commodification of labor, and about differential per-pupil expenditure on schools and differential access to health care rather than about the division of society into classes. (Rorty 1995: 212)

It is interesting to note that while such terms as capitalism and socialism may still be in use amongst academics in many countries around the world, in British politics they have been largely expunged from the vocabulary of the Labour party under the leadership of Neil Kinnock, John Smith, and Tony Blair.

## The beginning of education

Education has been a supreme element in human existence since time immemorial. Education as a major subject of study in higher education in England, however, has been of brief duration and low status. Joseph Payne, the first Professor of the Science and Art of Education in Britain, appointed to that position in 1873 by the College of Preceptors, a chartered body of teachers, was a man of humble origins without a university qualification. The majority of his students were prospective or practising female teachers in girls' secondary schools.

Payne's professorial lecture courses comprised 'The Science or Theory of Education', 'The Art or Practice of Education' and 'The History of Education'. He also conducted inspections of teaching in schools. The breadth of his interests and the esteem in which he was held are demonstrated by the roles he played in a variety of educational organizations: chairman of the Women's Education Union, chairman of the Philological Society, vice president of the College of Preceptors, vice president of the Scholastic Registration Association, council member of the Girls' Public Day School Company, committee member of the Froebel Society and chairman of the inaugural meeting of the Society for the Development of the Science of Education, founded in 1875. Payne believed that in his own day the science of education was in a very rudimentary condition, its basic principles scattered across a number of fields. He was also somewhat wary of a full-blown concept of a science of education, preferring the formulation 'science and art'. He believed that 'education has a basis of its own, and that basis is human nature' (quoted in Aldrich 1995: 217).

A further beginning of education in England may be associated with the establishment from the 1890s of day training facilities in connection with universities and university colleges. King's College, London, was amongst the first of these. The London Day Training College, founded in 1902, soon became the largest and most important. The subject of education in the day training colleges, however, was itself largely shaped by central directives. Since 1846 the education and training of pupil teachers had been strictly controlled by governments, which from the 1850s also prescribed curricula for teacher training colleges. In May 1890, under the terms of Circular 287, central government required that in the new institutions 'a normal master or mistress must be appointed to lecture on history and theory of education, to supervise teaching and to give a course of model lessons and preside at criticism lessons'. Most of the university trained students were destined to teach in elementary schools, a situation which continued until the second world war. Until the 1960s the majority of those who studied education as a subject would not attain a degree; indeed, some of those who taught them were non-graduates themselves. In the first half of the twentieth century, and beyond, where the subject of education was welcomed into universities it was frequently on practical rather than academic grounds, for intending teachers brought guaranteed funding.

Two examples of the problems associated with the status of education as a subject of study were provided by the universities of Oxford and Cambridge. Day training began in the two ancient universities in the 1890s, but Oxford refused to sanction the appointment of a single professor in the subject until 1989 (by which time this Institute had appointed 49) (Thomas 1990: 193-204), while in 1938 the first incumbent of a chair at Cambridge, G.R. Owst, accepted an appointment which he was to hold for 21 years on the understanding that he could continue with his medieval historical scholarship and not be too bothered with education (Searby 1982: 37).

This situation may be contrasted with that in German-speaking countries where educational science (Erziehungswissenschaft) was given formal recognition in the second half of the eighteenth century, with the first chair in the subject established at the University of Halle in Prussia in 1780 and another in Vienna in 1805. Nevertheless, even in these lands where educational science had a basis in philosophy as well as in pedagogy, problems were legion. As Heinz-Elmar Tenorth has concluded, progress was pitifully slow for a discipline which was 'Caught between profession and science, between research and politics, between practice and theory' (Tenorth 1995: 9).

The development of education as a university subject in England in the twentieth century has been reviewed by David Crook and myself in a chapter to be published this year in the third volume in the new ISCHE series. That chapter provides some account of achievements and failures, of gains and losses. It certainly indicates the leading roles played in the development of education by such Institute staff as its first two directors, John Adams and Percy Nunn, a theme to be considered in detail in the forthcoming centenary history of the Institute. But notwithstanding the contributions and international standing of such scholars, it must also be acknowledged that there have been many critics of education as an academic discipline or field of study. These include Fred Clarke, the third director of this Institute, who in 1943 declared that if other professions conducted public discussion in the same way as did educationists, then 'most patients would die, most bridges would fall down, and most manufacturing concerns would go bankrupt' (quoted in Oliver 1946: 10).

In 1994 Robert Skidelsky echoed this sentiment. In commenting on the immaturity of education with respect to disciplinary status, Skidelsky referred to 'its relative inability to generate uncontested propositions and its paucity of testable hypotheses . . . education is also immature in the sense that what ought to be questions of fact are too often turned into questions of interpretation' (*TES* 4 February 1994).

In 1996 David Hargreaves, in a lecture entitled 'Teaching as a research-based profession: possibilities and prospects', provided an explanation for this phenomenon, arguing that

> In medicine, as in the natural sciences, research has a broadly cumulative character . . . Much educational research is, by contrast, non-cumulative, in part because few researchers seek to create a body of knowledge which is then tested, extended or replaced in some systematic way. (Hargreaves 1996: 2)

Two comments may be made at this point. The first is that since education, like history, has some of the attributes both of a science and of an art, on occasion what appear to be questions of educational fact may indeed, become questions of educational interpretation. The second, that within the United Kingdom a more coherent approach both to the development of a discipline of education and to its connections with educational policies and practices, is urgently required. History of education, which can provide much of the data for a cumulative approach, and historical perspectives, have a vital role to play in this process.

Of course, viewed as an interaction between a discipline and a field of study, history of education may appear to differ little from other thematic approaches to history: for example those of politics, religion, diplomacy, female emancipation, naval warfare, none of which would claim to be a discipline in its own right. Nevertheless, even such comparisons from a thematic perspective, given the centrality of education in human experience across all periods and cultures, would seem to confirm the centrality of history of education among historical studies. Indeed, if, as argued in the previous section, one of the consequences of the end of history is to give a higher priority to such areas as education as opposed to other matters of state, history of education should itself assume a higher priority both in historical and in educational studies.

As yet, other factors have militated against such centrality, not least from the point of view of historians in general. Some of these reflect the purposes for which history has been studied and taught. For example, the central theme of school (and other) history has traditionally been that of high politics – monarchs, ministers, parliaments, wars, the promotion of a concept of leadership among the few, and of a shared consciousness of nation and nationhood among the many. In contrast, the subject of education has been perceived to be of less interest and of lower status. The early professors of history of education in British universities, scholars such as J.W. Adamson at King's College, London and Foster Watson at Aberystwyth University College, were distinguished historians by any standards. But the institutional contexts within which they and their colleagues worked, and the specific purposes to which their work was put, meant that history of education was often taught and studied as a means of promoting the identity and sense of mission of prospective and practising members of the teaching profession, rather than as a study of the past on its own terms, or as a central contribution to the broader historical education of the population.

It would appear that the perception that history is an academic discipline, with a broadly agreed set of procedures, while education is not, is particularly strong in England (Szreter 1989: 85-9). This situation may be contrasted with those in many other countries. As Marie-Madeleine Compère, in a comparative study of history of education textbooks in England, France, Germany, Ireland, Italy and Spain has shrewdly observed, in England 'education in its proper sense, however, has never enjoyed any great intellectual prestige and thus has no inertia to set against historical innovation, as might be the case if it possessed a prestigious tradition' (Compère 1993: 243). This is a most important point, albeit the term 'inertia' has somewhat negative connotations. In the context of my argument this evening, the phrase 'inertia to set against historical innovation', may be replaced by 'broadly agreed consensus as regards educational theory and practice to set against hasty, unwarranted or ideologically based innovation'.

## Conclusion

Two preliminary, and four further points may be made in conclusion. The preliminary points are essentially personal, 'present-minded' and 'ideologically positioned'.

The first is to reiterate my commitment to the importance of identifying ourselves – as individuals, as groups, as nations, as a human race – as accurately as possible in historical time. Such identification is as difficult as it is important. The difficulty is inherent in the complexity of the task. The importance stems from the power provided by such identification to maximize opportunities to promote the amounts of truth, justice, understanding and goodwill in the world.

The second point is to suggest that the best means of ensuring that such power is used for good rather than for evil purposes, is to be found in a firm commitment to a broad and generous interpretation of education. Such an interpretation certainly includes a concern for economic well being. But worthwhile education is also about the promotion of knowledge over ignorance, of truth over falsehood, of concern for others over selfishness, of effort over sloth, of mental and physical wellbeing over despair and debility.

The four further conclusions are drawn in respect of: the end of history, the beginning of education, the current and future agenda of historians of education, the particular role of this Institute.

The concept of the end of history is a valuable one, not least because it celebrates and strengthens the principles and practices of liberal democracies, whose governments, historically, have shown themselves less likely than other regimes to commit crimes either against their own peoples or against those of other countries. Of course, neither in history nor in historiography are there absolute ends and beginnings, except, perhaps, as delimited by the lives of individuals themselves. Interpretations such as the death of the past and the end of history, which remain committed to an objective search for truth, must be set against relativist and postmodernist approaches to create a professional and public historical consciousness of the past, present and future. Such consciousness is vital to the attainment and defence of liberal democracies. For the mythologies of the present and of the future are intimately connected with the mythologies of the past. Extended analysis of the concept of the end of history, moreover, is most appropriate as the human race comes to the close of one millennium and prepares to enter another. As the annual report from the Stockholm Institute for Peace has shown, although in the past two years there have been more than 20 internal conflicts, from Afghanistan to Rwanda, perhaps for the first time since records began there have been no major wars between states. It is salutary to reflect upon the many cruelties which have been perpetrated during the present century by some human beings upon others, in the pursuit of such ideologies as Imperialism, Fascism and Communism, to name but three. The current outbreak of peace provides an opportunity both to secure such a situation, and to address other global problems in a more determined and united manner than hitherto. The concept of the end of history may be linked with another notion, that of spaceship earth, of a planet whose life support systems, threatened by such factors as overpopulation, pollution and ozone depletion, must be preserved in the interests of the several species who inhabit it.

The concept of the beginning of education is similarly useful. Of course education has always been an important element in human existence, but at this particular point in time education as a subject of study and research in higher education in the United Kingdom has the potential for a new beginning, in the way in which other subjects, including history, probably do not. One basis for this new beginning is the enhanced profile of education upon the political agenda. Another is the increased participation rate in higher education, which has trebled in the last 20 years. Even more important is the concept of an increasing ownership of education by the whole community. In the light of such developments, Hargreaves' argument that a more productive relationship needs to be created between educational research and educational practice is a valid one, although his explanations as to the causes of the problem and the best means of solution are less convincing. Simply to castigate the educational research community (as Hargreaves does) for failing adequately to produce, co-ordinate and disseminate its findings is insufficient. It must also be acknowledged, for example, that governments, the media, teachers and parents in the United Kingdom have frequently been less receptive to such findings than similar groups in other countries. In recent years, political and economic ideology has been the mainspring for educational reform. Nevertheless, the opportunities and responsibilities for co-ordinating and disseminating the findings of research in education have never been greater. At times this may require educational researchers to stand up against governments or those agents of governments who seek to deny the truth. As Alexander Meiklejohn has written in the context of the academic freedom of professional researchers:

> those by whom we are commissioned need intellectual leadership in the thinking which a free society must do. May I state the principle bluntly and frankly? Our final responsibility, as scholars and teachers, is not to the truth. It is to the people who need the truth. (Quoted in Horio 1988: 393)

The role of historians of education in the development of education as a field of study and in the promotion of educational truths is crucial. Although in recent years the contexts and means of education have changed rapidly – for example as a result of the introduction of television and video, of computer and CD-Rom – and will no doubt continue to do so, there is a considerable corpus of knowledge about teaching and learning which does not alter. Good teachers combine a range of qualities – knowledge of their subjects, steady application of principles of management and organization, genuine concern for those whom they teach, the ability to inspire and enthuse. These qualities do not change over time. They need to be restated in every age, but their essence remains the same. Education is not susceptible to quick fixes, whether as a result of political intervention or pedagogical fashion. The role of the historian of education is to demonstrate continuities and changes, and to distinguish that which is important and long lasting from that which is shallow and transient. The privilege of working, as I do, in a History and Philosophy group whose agenda is international in scope, moreover, is that further perspectives are brought upon those elements in life which may be deemed to be worthwhile, elements which transcend both different cultures and different groups in multicultural societies. Richard Rorty wrote of banalizing discourse by using terms such as greed, selfishness, starvation wages, differential per-pupil expenditure. This is not banalizing. It is the proper language of historians of education, as of all historians and educationists.

Banality (or rather clarity) of language must be complemented by breadth of approach. Since its retreat from the 'undifferentiated mush' of the 1960s, there has been a problem in the field of education, a problem correctly identified by Hargreaves and others, of too many 'splitters' and not enough 'lumpers'. Historians of education and historical perspectives can provide solutions to this problem. Of course, as yet the historical perspectives approach in respect of education is at a relatively early stage of development. The balance between in-depth research on particular issues and general overviews has still to be struck. In a recent review of *Education for the Nation*, Tony Edwards argued that 'breadth too often defeats depth' (*TES* 6 December 1996). That may be a just comment on a volume which, in seeking to explain the overall issue of ownership of education in England from an historical perspective, considered seven fundamental themes: access, curriculum, standards and assessment, teaching quality, control of education, education and economic performance and educational consumers. Nevertheless, although each of these themes merits further detailed investigation in its own right, the importance of cumulative research which contributes to an extended body of knowledge is paramount.

My final point concerns the potential role of the Institute of Education in this process. In this lecture I have argued from the concepts of the end of history and of the beginning of education that an important opportunity now exists in this country to advance the true cause of education, both professional and public. For nearly a century, the Institute of Education of the University of London, and its predecessor until 1932 the London Day Training College, have been a central force for education, both nationally and internationally. This situation continues. In recent months such centrality has brought leading politicians, past and present – Paddy Ashdown, Kenneth Baker, Tony Blair, James Callaghan, Roy Hattersley and Gillian Shephard – to its lecture halls. The Institute's current authority and prestige rest upon a number of firm foundations. These include: the leadership of its director, Peter Mortimore; substantial library and archive collections; a top rating of five starred in yet another research assessment exercise, with no fewer than 140 scholars judged as being of international standing.

The Institute, therefore, is uniquely placed to provide leadership in education at this crucial time. Recent structural reforms, moreover, have facilitated the processes whereby specialized work in discrete areas of education may be brought into a cumulative whole. For example, my own understanding of such issues as education and employment and education and nationality have been much enhanced by the work of my colleague, John White (White 1996). Or again, this lecture is in one sense a discrete entity, as were those of Michael Barber and Geoff Whitty, delivered on 11 December 1996 and 9 January 1997 respectively. But it is also part of a series, and its connections with these two recent lectures are obvious, and may provide one basis for future collaboration. In *How to do the Impossible: a guide for politicians with a passion for education*, Michael Barber drew upon Fukuyama's concept of trust as expressed in his volume of that name, published in 1995 (Fukuyama 1995b). Geoff Whitty, in the Karl Mannheim Memorial Lecture entitled *Social Theory and Education Policy*, showed how sociologists of education, in common with many historians of education, have turned their attention to policy studies. Reference to his archival research about Mannheim, moreover, gave the lie to at least one half of the old aphorism that 'History is Sociology with the brains left out; Sociology is History with the hard work left out'.

An important recent study of the value and truth of historical knowledge has concluded that 'Telling the truth takes a collective effort' (Appleby, Hunt and Jacob 1994: 309). I believe this to be equally true of educational knowledge.

To return to the vision of Sidney Webb – 'The obvious and imperative duty of a rightly organised and adequately endowed London University is to become the foremost post-graduate centre of the intellectual world.' It is my earnest hope that this Institute will take full advantage of current opportunities to continue and to enhance its role as the foremost postgraduate centre in the intellectual world of education, and that such leadership will have a direct bearing upon educational policies and practice in the twenty-first century. I also hope that this lecture has made some contribution, however modest, towards that end.

# References

Aldrich, R. (1979), *Sir John Pakington and National Education*. Leeds: University of Leeds.

—     (1984), 'New history: an historical perspective'. In: A. Dickinson, P. Lee and P. Rogers (eds), *Learning History*. London: Heinemann Educational Books.

—     (1988), 'Imperialism in the study and teaching of history'. In J.A. Mangan (ed.), *'Benefits bestowed'? Education and British Imperialism*. Manchester: Manchester University Press.

—     (1990), 'The evolution of teacher education'. In: N. Graves (ed.), *Initial Teacher Education: Policies and Progress*. London: Kogan Page.

—     (ed) (1991), *History in the National Curriculum*. London: Kogan Page.

—     (1993), 'Discipline, practice and policy: a personal view of history of education'. In: K. Salimova and E. Johanningmeier (eds), *Why Should We Teach History of Education?*. Moscow: Rusanov Publishing House.

—     (1995), *School and Society in Victorian Britain: Joseph Payne and the New World of Education*. New York: Garland; Epping: College of Preceptors.

—     (1996), *Education for the Nation*. London: Cassell.

Aldrich, R. and Gordon, P. (1989), *Dictionary of British Educationists.* London: Woburn Press.

Aldrich, R. and Leighton, P. (1985), *Education: Time for a New Act?* London: Institute of Education.

Appleby, J., Hunt, L. and Jacob, M. (1994), *Telling the Truth about History.* New York: Norton.

Barber, M. (1996), *The Learning Game: Arguments for an Education Revolution.* London: Victor Gollancz.

Barnett, C. (1986), *The Audit of War.* London: Macmillan.

Brennan, E.J.T. (ed.) (1975), *Education for National Efficiency: the Contribution of Sidney and Beatrice Webb.* London: Athlone Press.

Centre for Contemporary Cultural Studies (1981), *Unpopular Education: Schooling and Social Democracy in England since 1944.* London: Hutchinson.

Clarke, P. (1992), 'Love's labours lost'. In: *History Today* (Introduction, A. Ryan), *After the End of History.* London: Collins and Brown.

Compère, M-M (1993), 'Textbooks on the history of education currently in use in Europe'. In: K. Salimova and E. Johanningmeier (eds), *Why Should We Teach History of Education?*. Moscow: Rusanov Publishing House.

Department for Education and Employment (1995), *The English Education System: an Overview of Structure and Policy.* London: DfEE.

Ferro, M. (1984), *The Use and Abuse of History, or, How the Past is Taught.* London: Routledge and Kegan Paul.

Frijhoff, W. (1996), 'Education's memory'. In: J. Sturm, J. Dekker, R. Aldrich and F. Simon (eds), *Education and Cultural Transmission*. Gent: C.S.H.P.

Fukuyama, F. (1989), 'The End of History?', *National Interest 16*, 3-18.

—     (1992), *The End of History and the Last Man*. London: Hamish Hamilton.

—     (1995a), 'On the possibility of writing a universal history'. In: A.M. Melzer, J. Weinberger and M.R. Zinman (eds), *History and the Idea of Progress*. Ithaca: Cornell University Press.

—     (1995b), *Trust: The Social Virtues and the Creation of Prosperity*. London: Hamish Hamilton.

Gordon, P. (ed.) (1980), *The Study of Education. A Collection of Inaugural Lectures: Early and Modern*. London: Woburn Press.

Gordon, P. and Aldrich, R. (1997), *Biographical Dictionary of North American and European Educationists*. London: Woburn Press.

Gordon, P., Aldrich, R. and Dean. D. (1991), *Education and Policy in England and Wales in the Twentieth Century*. London: Woburn Press.

Handy, C., (1996) 'What's it all for? Reinventing capitalism for the next century', *Royal Society of Arts Journal, CXLIV 5475*, 33-40.

Hargreaves, D.H. (1996), 'Teaching as a Research-Based Profession: Possibilities and Prospects'. Teacher Training Agency Annual Lecture 1996.

Horio, T. (edited and translated by Steven Platzer) (1988), *Educational Thought and Ideology in Modern Japan: State Authority and Intellectual Freedom*. Tokyo: University of Tokyo Press.

Jenkins, K. (1995), *On 'What is History?' From Carr and Elton to Rorty and White*. London: Routledge.

Keynes, J.M. (1926), *The End of Laissez Faire*. London: Hogarth.

Laqueur, T.W. (1976), *Religion and Respectability: Sunday Schools and Working-Class Culture 1780-1850*. New Haven: Yale University Press.

Oliver, R.A.C. (1946), *Research in Education*. London: Allen and Unwin.

Plumb, J.L. (1969), *The Death of the Past*. London: Macmillan.

Popkewitz, T.K. (1991), *A Political Sociology of Educational Reform*. New York: Teachers College.

Rorty, R. (1995), 'The end of Leninism and history as comic frame'. In: A.M. Melzer, J. Weinberger and M.R. Zinman (eds), *History and the Idea of Progress*. Ithaca: Cornell University Press.

Searby, P. (1982), *The Training of Teachers in Cambridge University: the First Sixty Years, 1879-1939*. Cambridge: Cambridge University Department of Education.

Sharp, P. (1995), *School Governing Bodies in the English Education System: an Historical Perspective*. Leeds: University of Leeds.

Szreter, R. (1989), 'History and the Sociological Perspective in Educational Studies'. In: P. Gordon and R. Szreter (eds), *History of Education: the Making of a Discipline*. London: Woburn Press.

Tenorth, H-E. (1995), 'Geschichte der Erziehungswissenschaft: Konstruktion einer Chimäre oder Historie einer Karriere?'. Paper delivered to the seventeenth congress of the International

Standing Conference for the History of Education, Berlin, September 1995. To be published in the conference volume of selected papers in 1997.

Thatcher, M. (1993), *The Downing Street Years*. London: Harper Collins.

Thomas, J.B. (ed.) (1990), *British Universities and Teacher Education: a Century of Change*. London: Falmer Press.

West, E.G. (1970), *Education and the State: a Study in Political Economy*. London: Institute of Economic Affairs.

White, J. (1996), 'Education and Nationality', *Journal of Philosophy of Education, 30 (3),* 327-43.

Wiener, M.J. (1981), *English Culture and the Decline of the Industrial Spirit, 1850-1980*. Cambridge: Cambridge University Press.